Revising Weddings

by
Charles Read

Priest-in-charge of St. James, Higher Broughton and St. Clement with St.
Matthias, Lower Broughton, Salford (from July 1994)

GROVE BOOKS LIMITED
Bramcote Nottingham NG9 3DS

Contents

Acknowledgements

My interest in this subject stems from my attending the Roman Catholic national liturgical conference in Guildford in 1990. I am grateful to Jennifer Demoulder and others responsible for this conference for the hospitality which they showed me.

Many patient audiences have listened to parts of this booklet and I am happy to record my thanks for their indulgence and their comments. Chief among these groups are students on the Northern Ordination Course, colleagues in Stretford deanery, fellow members of the Cuming Seminar at Manchester University and, especially, friends in the Group for the Renewal of Worship. I am especially grateful to Trevor Lloyd, Tim Stratford, Jane Sinclair, Michael Vasey and Phillip Tovey for their help.

I must also record my thanks to my wife, Judith, who word-processed it all (except this bit!).

The Cover Picture is by Peter Ashton.

First Impression April 1994.
ISSN 0305-3067
ISBN 1 85174 263 8

1
Lessons from History

Most clergy's experience of weddings is that the couple appears at church on what we hope is a fine Saturday afternoon, we perform the ceremony and the wedding party retires for the reception which may last late into the night. While the festivities are going on, the clergyman may have performed one or more other wedding ceremonies. In many places it has long since ceased to be customary to invite the Vicar back to the wedding reception.

The congregation which habitually worships in the church may never have seen the couple at all. Banns will probably have been called and the couple may have attended the reading of them, but it is often the case that weddings are seen as something which the clergy do rather than a ministry of the whole congregation.

It was not always quite like this. Up until the ninth century, the betrothal would take place in the home as would the marriage ceremony itself. Getting married was a domestic and civil affair and specifically Christian elements were only introduced gradually. 'Christians marry, like everybody else' we find written in the letter of Diognetus in the late second century. Gradually, clergy were expected to seek the bishop's blessing on their marriages, but it was only in the ninth century (in the West) that people began to come to church for a Mass with nuptial blessing, preceded by a domestic betrothal and followed by further domestic rites.

From the twelfth century onwards, the betrothal and consent took place at the church door, followed by the Mass with nuptial blessing and then there were domestic rites at home, including the blessing of the bridal bed! It seems, though, that only the wealthier classes really availed themselves of the church's ministrations and this was to protect 'their' women and children. Thus, while marriage rites can be found for the middle ages, not everyone used them.[1]

With the Reformation, marriage in England became a church affair and the domestic rites disappeared. It was envisaged by Cranmer in 1549 and 1552 that Holy Communion would conclude a marriage service. However, by 1662 the recommendation for Communion to follow is reduced to a hope that Communion might follow.[2] By 1980, the ASB merely suggests a way of combining marriage and Communion services.

The Roman Catholics in England found that, in the eighteenth and nineteenth centuries, they had to have the betrothal and marriage ceremonies in an Anglican church and could then have a Mass with nuptial blessing at a Catholic Church.[3] (Since 1753 marriages could only legally be contracted in Anglican churches, the only exceptions being for Quakers and Jews.)

This situation changed in the nineteenth century so that the same procedure (marriage followed by nuptial Mass) could take place in a Roman Catholic Church. At

---

[1] The most useful collection of documents is by K. Stevenson and M. Searle *Documents of the Marriage Liturgy* (Pueblo 1992). See especially p. 260.

[2] See the Everyman edition of the Edwardine Prayer Books, pp. 258 and 416.

[3] Sometimes the Catholic ceremonies were *followed* by Anglican ones, and often Catholic couples refused to go on to the parish church: see O. Chadwick *The Victorian Church* (A & C Black 1970) vol. 1 pp.142ff.

the same time, Nonconformists were allowed to marry in their own chapels - though they had not felt so put out at the previous obligation to be married in the parish church since they often had some connection there already. (This was especially true of Methodists.) Unitarians were, however, the exception as they had objected to being married under trinitarian formulae - and Anglican clergy had been unhappy to use such formulae over couples who plainly disbelieved them!

The Roman Catholic system from 1970 onwards provided for a marriage ceremony embedded in a nuptial Mass: the liturgy of the word is followed by the marriage and this then leads into the eucharist with nuptial blessing. All of this of course takes place in a church setting.[1]

The Free Churches have provided wedding services which are similar in structure to Anglican ones. The Methodist Church order suggests that communion may conclude the service but there is not even a mention of this possibility in the latest Baptist resource book for worship. This probably only reflects attitudes towards the frequency of communion in the various Free Churches.

The main lesson to learn from this historical sketch is that marriage has not always taken place exclusively in a church. Indeed, in the early Middle Ages people often simply lived together without finding any need to come to church for a wedding. This may give us a clue about how to regard the status of people who co-habit in our society today. Are they really married, or are they 'living in sin'? [2]

In 1990, the Roman Catholic Liturgical Conference for England and Wales met in Guildford to consider some proposals for revising their marriage rites. I was one of the observers at that conference and much of what follows in this booklet stems from some of the proposals put forward there. One of the things which the committee which drew up these new proposals tried to do was to draw on the insights of Christian history concerning marriage ceremonies, and particularly to move away from seeing getting married as something which happened in half an hour on a Saturday afternoon in July.

My aim here is to suggest ways of revising the marriage rites (especially in the ASB), drawing on the insights from history and especially in the light of the proposed revisions by the Roman Catholic Church in England and Wales. The purpose of such revision is to meet what are perceived to be contemporary needs and to enrich the marriage service for its own sake. There is a feeling that church weddings are becoming increasingly dominated by elements other than the service and its meaning. Can the Christian Church do anything to reclaim weddings from the often romanticized affairs they seem to have become?

1 A fuller history of marriage rites can be found in Kenneth Stevenson's two books: *Nuptial Blessing* (SPCK 1982) and *To Join Together* (Pueblo 1987).
2 See the recent ethical discussion in Gary Jenkins *Cohabitation: a Biblical perspective* (Grove Ethical Studies No. 84), Jeremy Collingwood *Common Law Marriage* (Grove Ethical Studies No. 93) and Ted Pratt *Living in Sin?* (available from Grove Books). See also Charles Read *Will you marry me?* in *News of Liturgy* 213 (Sept. 1992).

2.
Theological and Ethical Questions

Before we can consider the revision of the ASB marriage service, there are some prior questions to be asked, since the Church of England has got itself into a position of uncertainty on some issues and is simply out of touch with reality on others. In addition, there are questions which have not been addressed explicitly before which need airing.

1. What constitutes getting married?

This question is a slippery one because when some people ask it it means 'What constitutes Christian marriage?', whereas other people want to ask the question 'How can you tell if a couple are really married?'

One way of approaching this issue is to ask the question: who is/are the minister(s) of the sacrament?[1] The classic Western view is that the couple marry each other. To use the language of sacraments, they are the ministers of the sacrament to each other. This makes the consent an important element and a reference such as Genesis 2.24 ('...a man will leave his father and mother and be united to his wife, and they will become one flesh') might be seen to undergird this view of marriage. Pushed a little further, this approach might enable us to say that a co-habiting couple are married if they are living in what they perceive to be a stable and lasting relationship, in that they have consented to leave their parental homes and have set up home together.

This is certainly the view taken by some clergy and was in part what led St. Augustine's Derby, in 1987, to offer 'free weddings' to co-habiting couples.[2] The situation was that a number of couples were living in the parish who had not been through a church or register office ceremony because they could not afford what they saw as the necessary 'big wedding'. No doubt they had been unduly influenced by seeing such things as royal weddings on T.V., but they, like many couples nowadays, thought that a proper wedding involved a lot of fuss and expense. In order to show that this need not be the case, and that we, as Christians, wanted to affirm them, rather than castigate them for living in sin, we offered to perform wedding services without charging any fees. This was subject to the usual legal requirements, was just for one Saturday in October, and couples had to go through the usual wedding preparations.

The experience in this inner-city parish revealed that getting married cannot be separated from wider issues of justice and righteousness. Housing laws, benefits procedures etc. sometimes force a couple to co-habit, or at least encourage them to do so, so that we cannot take the moral high ground and denounce co-habitation without addressing the pressures which push couples into such a situation.

The history of wedding services also sheds light on this. For centuries, there was no compulsion for Christians to seek a 'church wedding' and cohabitation was not just

---

1 I do not wish to assume that it is appropriate to talk of marriage as a sacrament, but I use the word in this context as part of a useful piece of shorthand!

2 See an article written by the Vicar: 'Free Weddings' by Mike Parsons, *(Church Times)* ninth Oct. 1987 page 5. I was a student on placement in the parish at the time.

tolerated - it was the norm. Mark Searle points out that the devout would seek the blessing of their new life together by a priest, but that this had a similar status to the blessing of a house today - a good idea (which more people might take up) but usually only sought by the keenest of Christians. What made a marriage *Christian,* he notes, was the fact the couple was baptized: 'the sacramentality of marriage as a state, depended not on a wedding rite but on the baptismal identity of the couple. Their life together was a form of the Christian life, a form which, in the mutual love and recip-rocal service for which marriage afforded occasion, was capable of iconicizing the mutual relationship between Christ and the Church.'[1]

History again shows that the (secular) Roman view was that consent was what made a relationship a marriage, whereas the Germanic tribes held cohabitation to be that which made a marriage. When the Roman Empire collapsed and these two groups intermingled, the lawyers put consent and cohabitation together to form the legal and social basis for marriage.[2]

There is, however, a second view of what constitutes getting married. It is often described as the Eastern view and is sometimes caricatured as a priest being essen-tial for a wedding and as the priest marrying the couple. This is not strictly speaking accurate - God is seen to marry the couple through the ministry of the priest. The parallel is drawn with the eucharist, where God consecrates the elements through the ministry of the priest. The Biblical basis for seeing the priest's role at weddings in this way lies in such passages as Ephesians 5.22ff, where marriage is seen as a mystery, in the same way that Christ's relationship with the Church is a mystery.[3] There is therefore a stress on the crowning in Eastern ceremonies. Eastern rites do not have a nuptial blessing and the crowning is their liturgical equivalent. In the West, the emphasis has usually been more on the consent of the couple. Western rites did develop nuptial blessings (i.e. in practice blessings of the bride) but the West has never been so insistent on the ministrations of a priest for a wedding to be deemed valid. Sometimes church people got a little worried about this: so, for example, Melchior Cano in the sixteenth century developed a theory that the couple's consent was the **'matter'** of the sacrament and the priestly blessing was the **'form'** of the sacrament. Thus using the medieval distinction between form and matter in sacraments, he devised a theory whereby people could validly marry and yet not receive the **sacra-ment** of marriage.

The problem with a view such as this, that places a lot of emphasis on the role of the priest/church, is that it does not seem to fit easily with marriage seen as a covenant between two people or marriage as a creation ordinance. The patriarchs in Genesis did not go through a marriage ceremony - they simply co-habited (on the basis of the principle outlined in Genesis 2.24). It does, however, point to the need for some public recognition that a marriage is taking place. The problem with co-habitation is that there is no public ceremony associated with it. No-one need know that a couple has begun to co-habit, even if a large furniture van is parked outside the house for most of the day. Marriage is not a private affair; it has a public dimension.

Kenneth Stevenson[4] suggests that both the consent and nuptial blessing should be

1 In M. Searle and K. Stevenson *op. cit.* (Pueblo 1992) p.253.
2 *Ibid.* pp.257ff.
3 See for example J. Meyendorff *Marriage: An Orthodox Perspective* (St. Vladimir's Seminary Press 1984) p.18ff.
4 M. Perham (Ed.), *Liturgy for a New Century,* (SPCK 1991) Ch. 6

the twin foci of getting married. This kind of di-polar view of what is happening in a wedding service would seem to combine the best of both approaches. The nuptial blessing, often framed as a thanksgiving prayer, is important because, if marriage is a gift from God, then we should thank him for it along with his other gifts. (This does not mean that weddings which do not include a clear nuptial blessing are invalid - to ask that question is too legalistic anyway - the desire some people have for Anglican weddings to include a clearer nuptial blessing is because Christian weddings should be as Christian as possible).

2. What is the heart of the wedding service?

In the village where I grew up, you would often hear people say 'I just want to see him put that ring on her finger.' This represents the popular view of what is at the heart of a wedding service: the ring-giving ceremony. (The BCP words 'with this ring I thee wed' are performative, or at least they appear to be, and so it is not difficult to see how this popular view arose). In fact, the ring is an illustration of the fact of marriage and the current Roman Catholic proposals, unveiled at the Guildford conference in 1990, move the exchange of rings well away from the heart of the marriage service and into a block of 'illustrative rituals'.

The divergent views of what constitutes getting married, outlined above, would lead us to say that the heart of the marriage rite in the West has been the consent, while in the East it has been the crowning. It may be argued that the consent constitutes the **theological** heart of getting married on the Genesis 2.24 model, if we are talking about marriage as something in which people in general participate. However a Christian couple would doubtless want to see the blessing of their marriage by God as significant. Christian tradition in the East has tended to stress that Christian marriage is of a different kind from Jewish or Roman (= secular) marriage and what makes a marriage Christian is not just that it is two Christians who are getting married, but that God performs their wedding through the ministry of the priest. Stevenson's attempt at a di-polar view may be helpful here, because it attempts to combine both these elements.

Nonetheless, the question remains of how to handle the popular view, that the ring-giving is the heart of the wedding, in a positive way. It is a symbol which couples would almost certainly not want to discard. The Roman Catholic Church in England and Wales suggests that the ring-giving should be put with a block of other symbolism, later in the service than the vows. It labels all such symbols 'illustrative'. This begs the question of whether symbols are merely illustrative and it may confuse symbols with signs. The words that accompany the symbol are significant if its meaning is not to be misunderstood: the American Episcopal Church has the words 'I give you this ring as a symbol of my vow' as opposed to the ASB's 'sign of my marriage'. The difference could be quite significant.

3. What theological themes are appropriate?

The ASB wedding service is very Christocentric, drawing on the story of the wedding at Cana etc. In this it is unlike other ASB services which have a greater emphasis on such themes as the Holy Spirit and the Church. The notion of marriage as covenant comes out in Roman Catholic approaches to marriage but could be stressed more in the ASB (or its successor).

Marriage is a creation ordinance and so you do not need to be a Christian in order to get married - you just need to have been created. (That is, in the second creation story in Genesis the man and the woman are put together by God as part of, or at least following on from, the creation of the world.) We might be tempted to think that it should therefore be possible for the Church to offer a marriage service based on a creation theology, but committed Christians would surely want a service which embodied themes of God's blessing through Christ, of a common married life together in Christ and so on. Added to which, the Christian church should surely be in the business of offering Christian wedding services. Some people have suggested there ought to be different services for Christians and non-Christians on the basis of the Anglican pastoral model of ministering to all in the parish regardless of religious affiliation. Once again, we minister as a Christian church and while we should seek to minister to all, we should not hide our identity in doing so. In any case, the distinctions between believers and non-believers are not always so clear-cut. Many couples who come to be married and who take no habitual part in the life and worship of the Church do have some sort of faith and belief in Christ, even if it is a long way from fully orthodox Christian faith. What is needed is a marriage service which is genuinely Christian but is also more flexible for different pastoral contexts.

Roman Catholic treatments of marriage can still tend to be rather legalistic, interpreting covenant and vow in a legal way. Such an approach can creep into Anglican marriage preparation where the legal elements which clergy are responsible for can predominate, especially if there are legal complications involving, for example, an Archbishop's Licence. The notion of marriage as a gift from God is a helpful corrective to such tendencies.

4. What is the status of the bride?

The wedding is often referred to as 'the bride's day' and this unwittingly alludes to an element within the history of marriage services. Women have been portrayed as goods to be passed to a new owner. Nuptial blessings have often been blessings of the bride only. This is because it is obvious that the bride is changing her status but it is not so obvious that the groom is changing his status. (The bride takes the groom's name and becomes a member of his household).

Other traditional elements which reflect this notion include the bride arriving with her father and having a grand entrance procession (while the groom has slipped quietly into church 15 minutes previously). The giving away is a particularly feudal ceremony, denoting more clearly than anything else that the bride is her father's property and is now being handed over to become someone else's property.[1] When I explain the origins of this custom to brides they are horrified, but they all want to keep it in the service!

In some cultures in Britain there is even the sense that it is the bride's day because she has 'won', that is 'got her husband' - the implication being that the groom is somewhat reluctant to get married. While this attitude may be conveyed in a joking way, I feel it is important for wedding liturgies to reflect the fact that both parties are willingly consenting to marriage and that what we are about is something joyful rather than an act of semi-coercion.

---

1 Most explicitly perhaps in the mediaeval southern French rites, where the priest says to the groom 'I hand her over to you'. See Stevenson and Searle *op. cit. p.13*.

Stevenson suggests that both the bride and the groom could be given away by sponsors (a parallel to baptism), which could include the bride's father but would also include some comparable person on the groom's side (maybe the best man).

Where a couple have been married in a register office, it is usual for them to process up the aisle together if they are having a blessing in church. We have seen, in the historical sketch, that part of the wedding ceremony used to take place at the church door. Maybe one way to deal with the question of the status of the bride is to have the wedding begin at the church door with questions to the couple about their intent to marry and then a wedding procession to the front of church for the rest of the service. The bride and groom could walk with each other or with their sponsors but, either way, it avoids the dramatic entrance of the bride alone which only reinforces the idea that it is the bride's day and not the couple's day. The bride could even have arrived at the church in the usual way (including being late!) to be met there by the groom. Traditional wedding music could still be used for the procession. Again, the Roman Catholic proposals include ideas such as this.

5. Divorce and Remarriage

There are two questions here, namely the ethical one of who (if anyone) qualifies for remarriage after divorce and the liturgical one of how such a marriage is celebrated. It is to be hoped that the current Church of England muddle on remarriage will soon be resolved. As it is, it is up to the conscience of individual clergy whether they will perform such ceremonies or not. Practices can vary widely from church to church. For example, I have found myself in a strange situation, since I am perfectly happy in principle to remarry divorcees but served my first curacy with an incumbent who was set against such a practice, and therefore, we did not accept divorcees for remarriage at all, although some of our regular congregation were themselves divorced and remarried. I then moved (for my second curacy) to a parish where we did remarry divorcees, after making careful enquiry into the breakdown of the first marriage. The (then) Bishop of Manchester's guideline was that we should not conduct a marriage where this new relationship had contributed to the breakdown of the first marriage. Other dioceses have other guidelines. We were strict in only accepting candidates where at least one partner lived in the parish. It is therefore unfortunate if you live in a parish where divorcees are not remarried. Geography and not theology determines whether divorcees may be remarried in the Church of England.

Where divorced people are getting married again, it is often suggested that a penitential element be introduced into the service, as a mark of repentance for the failure of the first marriage. This is a laudable thing to do and I find that many divorced people seeking a remarriage deeply regret their part in the breakdown of their former marriage. The question is, how do you do this in the context of a marriage service?

A confession for everyone to take part in can be rather strange where the bride for example has not been married before. Why should her prospective husband's divorce prevent her from having a straightforward wedding service? Some divorced people have therefore had a public confession before the arrival of the bride or at another service (e.g. the Sunday before). The Church of the Province of Southern Africa has a special introduction to a marriage service for divorced persons which is strongly penitential. It includes the following:

'A Christian marriage is both a civil contract and spiritual union....It is a serious matter to break a civil contract. It is a much more serious matter to break a vow which one has made for life before God....

The Bishop himself is satisfied that in this instance there is no prospect of re-establishing a true marriage relationship between the partners of the former marriage(s). N and N have been interviewed and the Bishop is assured that there is due penitence for the failure of the previous marriage(s) and a knowledge of God's forgiveness as well as a readiness to forgive....

St. John says: 'If we say we have no sin, we deceive ourselves, and the truth is not in us. If we confess our sins, God is just, and may be trusted to forgive our sins and cleanse us from every kind of wrong'.

We all need to know the forgiving and healing power of God's love, for God's forgiveness brings healing of all the hurts of the past which sin has inflicted.

Let us therefore together ask God's pardon. Then, in the joy of his forgiveness, we can ask his blessing on the marriage of N and N.'[1]

The Eastern Orthodox marriage liturgy also includes a penitential note for remarriage after divorce, even stronger than that in the South African rite. Orthodox couples may not have a wedding in the context of a eucharist if one of them has been divorced.[2] (And Basil the Great, in the fourth century, makes the same prohibition with regard to remarriage after widowhood - which meant that such marriages could only be contracted as civil agreements, since there was no non-eucharistic church wedding service then.)

Such a strong penitential statement is probably too much for most occasions but the present marriage service lacks any form of confession at all and maybe this is an omission which could be corrected.[3] A paragraph which spoke of God's forgiveness would not come amiss if it acknowledged that a divorce had taken place.

3.
Staging and Structure

The Roman Catholic Church in England and Wales is in the process of revising its wedding ceremonies. I propose to use their suggested revisions to focus attention on some of the changes which could be made to the ASB wedding service (or to any wedding service).

The usual scenario for a church wedding is that the couple turn up on the day and the ceremony is performed. In most parishes, the couple will have been through some form of preparation for marriage, their banns will have been read and they may have been prayed for at the main Sunday service.

After the marriage service, the couple are often not seen in church again until they want their baby baptized! However, the process of getting married has, for them, been much more drawn out and complicated than this. They have met each other and got

---

1 *A South African Prayer Book* pp. 484f.
2 See Meyendorff, *op. cit.* p.45 for details of this service.
3 The Methodist Service Book does include the possibility of a (general) confession at the start of the service - see p.E6.

engaged, their respective families have met each other, they have made preparations for wedding receptions and a honeymoon, and after the wedding ceremony (if not before) they will move into their new home and begin to settle into married life. There will be significant milestones along the way such as anniversaries, and the birth of children.

The fact that the church is only involved in a small part of this process, even for committed Christian couples, means that many people see the church part of getting married as relatively unimportant and insignificant. This comes out fairly clearly when couples complain about what they think are exorbitant wedding fees. There has thus been a desire to reclaim weddings for the church lest they become entirely secular spectaculars with a church component lost somewhere in the middle. Part of the process of reclaiming weddings has been to advocate a staged or phased approach to getting married.

'Phased rites' are usually linked with some understanding of the anthropologist van Gennep's *Les Rites de Passage*.[1] He observed that initiation rites are made up of three stages: separation, liminality and incorporation. (Separation and incorporation are fairly obvious; liminality is that stage where the person is preparing for the change that is coming - for example the catechumenate in initiation). The Roman Catholic RCIA (Rites of Christian Initiation of Adults) took this on board with its stress on adult baptism / confirmation as a process, and hence its revival of the catechumenate. There then followed the Order of Christian Funerals (OCF) which applied the same system to funerals and the attendant rites (e.g. prayers with the dying, interment of ashes).

The proposals for a new Roman Catholic marriage service for England and Wales have applied the same approach to getting married.[2] The thinking behind this is:

(a) to reclaim weddings from the secular realm
(b) to reflect what actually happens to couples in practice - that they go through a many-staged process leading up to the wedding and continuing after it
(c) to demonstrate the church's concern with all aspects of getting married and not just the marriage rite itself
(d) to underline that you do not 'get married' on a particular day - marriage is a life-long and continual process which is not completed in one service.

The scheme has a three stage structure:

(i)   engagement;
(ii) marriage;
(iii) renewals and anniversaries.

It may include prayers and ceremonies at home as well as at church. The way this breaks down is as follows:

public/church	*private/home*
engagement	meals with family
	preparation groups
wedding	reception
	blessing of new home
anniversaries	
reconciliations	

1 A. van Gennep *Les Rites de Passage* (Paris 1909).
2 At the time of writing, the texts are only available in a limited number of draft forms. Official publication is likely to be no sooner than 1995.

11

The result is that provision is made for a wide variety of different prayers and services. The compilers realize that not every couple will opt for the complete set of services and it will take a while for some of the new ideas to gain currency. However, it is not unusual in Anglican circles for couples to be prayed for when their banns are read and I recently came across one church which had a simple anointing ceremony carried out when the couple come to book the wedding. The Roman Catholic proposals are of course much more complex than this and a summary of them may help to give an idea of what could be done.

Staged Rites
What follows is a brief outline of the various stages or phases proposed in the new Roman Catholic Marriage Rites. I defer a discussion of the actual Mass for weddings until later.

1. Engagement
There are two parts to the provision for engagement: one is a celebration of the engagement and the other material for use during the period of preparation for getting married.

(a) The rite for celebrating engagement may take place in the home or in church. It includes the lighting of family candles (of which more in the next chapter) and the reading of scripture verses. There is opportunity for the couple to pray, for the peace to be exchanged and for food and drink to be blessed (in the home version of the rite). Perhaps the central part is the blessing of the couple and the engagement ring.

The church version of this rite is fuller in that it includes an expanded ministry of the word and scope for music and songs as well as more prayers.

(b) The material for the preparation period includes suggestions for worship components in marriage preparation groups (setting the preparation session in a liturgical context much as happens with RCIA). There is also material which could be used when the families share meals (and the family candles appear again!) There are suggestions for prayers which a family may use with one of its members who is to be married and finally there is material which can be used at the Sunday Mass where engaged couples can be blessed or when the wedding itself will not be a nuptial Mass and one or both partners want a eucharistic dimension to their getting married.

2. Marriage
The wedding liturgy may be within Mass or outside it. The shape of the wedding service, as now proposed, is quite different from the current nuptial Mass (or indeed any existing wedding service), and I will discuss this below. In the section headed 'Marriage', there are also to be found prayers provided as grace for the wedding reception and there is provision for the blessing of a new home, possibly in a eucharistic context. The historical precedent for this latter service is actually the medieval blessing of the bed-chamber, now extended to the whole house!

The blessing of the house includes a reading chosen from a list of passages which

relate to homes. There is then a set of prayers for use in each room of the house and these may be accompanied by the sprinkling of holy water. There is the possibility of this degenerating into unwarranted merriment, but the prayers provided try hard to avoid this. For example, the bedroom prayer reads:
> 'Protect us, Lord, while we are awake;
> watch over us as we sleep,
> that awake we may keep watch with Christ,
> and asleep we may rest in his peace.'[1]

The wedding candle (of which more later) is then lit and, if the Christian community has given the couple a gift, this can be installed in its place. What is envisaged here is that a Bible may be placed on the bookshelf or a crucifix nailed to the wall. It is not envisaged that the congregation will have bought the couple a washing machine which is ceremoniously plumbed in at this stage! Presumably in such a case provision could be made for blessing the water as well....

The service ends with prayers and a blessing. The eucharistic version of the service is very similar with the eucharist being celebrated in a simple way in a suitable room in the house.

3. Anniversaries, renewals and reconciliations

The idea here is to enable people to celebrate wedding anniveraries either in the home or in church. The domestic setting may be that of a Mass or a family meal. The wedding candle features yet again and the couple can renew their commitment to each other. There is also a rite for celebrating renewal in church within Mass. This is envisaged as a group celebration (i.e. several couples renewing vows together) but follows similar lines to the anniversary material.

Provision has been made for family reconciliations which can be used where families have been split up for some reason (maybe one partner has been working away from home for a long period or the marriage has hit a rocky patch and there has been a separation). There may be confession and absolution in this service.

Reading the book of proposals which the Roman Catholic Church in England and Wales has produced may leave the impression that they envisage prayers for every possible occasion. Indeed, at the conference at which this scheme was launched, a group of nuns with whom I was having lunch suggested that what the book lacked was a set of prayers for the blessing of a ladder prior to elopement. Presumably the scripture reading would be the story of Jacob's vision of the ladder to heaven.

In fact, as I mentioned above, few, if any, couples will use all of the material. Clergy will have to be selective and pastorally sensitive in commending the material to couples. I believe that Anglicans (and others) can introduce this staged or phased approach to marriage in a low-key way, perhaps by praying for couples who are to be married if they come to hear their banns read. The couple could be asked to stand up where they are or come out to the front. Christian families can be encouraged to pray for members who are to be married as part of a revival of prayer in the home. The renewal of marriage vows and wedding anniversary services already happen in some places. Seen in this light, the Roman Catholic suggestions do not seem so bizarre.

---

1 Though it must be admitted that wedding liturgies are not very good at recognizing the sexual aspect of marriage, apart from coy references (as in the ASB) or the BCP's 'brute beasts'!

13

The Wedding Service Itself

In addition to providing a set of staged rites, the Roman Catholics have restructured the wedding service itself to reflect their thinking on some of the issues I have discussed in chapter two. Much of what they suggest is in line with Kenneth Stevenson's suggestions for revising the ASB marriage service, which is hardly surprising since he acted as advisor to those who drew up the Roman Catholic Proposals. The wedding Mass proceeds as follows:

1. Introductory rites

The priest meets the couple at the church door and leads them inside the church. The congregation stands and faces the wedding party. The priest greets the people and it is envisaged that the first part of the service takes place at the church door. This is an attempt to include the bride and groom on an equal level and to symbolize their coming to church as a couple to be married. Of course, as I suggested earlier, the groom may have arrived early and the bride may have arrived in the usual way but to be met by the groom at the door and not at the front of church.

There is a brief opening address about why the people are gathered together on this occasion and then the priest asks the couple how they understand marriage. This takes the form of a statement by the priest, followed by a question ('Is this how you understand marriage, and intend to live it?') to which the couple simply reply 'It is'.

The priest then asks: 'Is it after due consideration and of your own free choice that you wish to enter into marriage?' Again the couple reply 'It is'.

The priest then asks if anyone present knows of any legal reason why the couple may not marry. There is then the declaration of intent:

'N, will you take N to be your wife/husband?

Will you love her/him, comfort her/him, honour and protect her/him, and, forsaking all others, be faithful to her/him as long as you both shall live?'.

The couple each reply in turn 'I will'.

An innovation[1] is that there is then a question to the families asking them if they will support the couple. (This question may be omitted for pastoral reasons). There is also a question to the congregation, asking them for their support. There then follows a prayer for the couple.

It is at this point that there is an entrance procession to the front of church. (It may be suggested that this is not strictly an *entrance* procession as the preceding questioning will have taken place at the back of church in most buildings, but there is no reason why there should not be a procession to the chancel step at this point.) This may, of course, use traditional music but again the point is that the couple go up the aisle together (though maybe accompanied by their sponsors if the Stevenson model is followed or by the bride's father and the best man or accompanying each other). If wedding candles are to be used in the service, the two family candles are lit at this point.

2. The Liturgy of the Word

In the Roman Catholic proposals, this is straightforward and is drawn from the stan-

---

1 It is an innovation for Catholics, and would be in the Church of England, but the Canadian *Book of Alternative Services* has it (p.531) as do the URC Service Book (1989) (p.54) and the Baptist *Patterns and Prayers for Christian Worship* (OUP 1991) (p.128).

dard lectionary. Stevenson, however, suggests making explicit the setting of the wedding in the context of salvation history by having the couple come forward to say 'I will' and then returning to their seats for the ministry of the word, coming forward again for the vows. This is pretty much what happens in the Roman Catholic proposal but, of course, in that the first part of the service has taken place at the church door.

The ASB is ambiguous about where its Ministry of the Word is to come. It may come early in the service or in the middle, before the prayers. Stevenson points out[1] that the shape of the ASB marriage service is messy because the Ministry of the Word and the registration can come in different places. This gives a number of variable forms to the marriage service and he feels it would be more helpful simply to have one form. The Roman Catholics have opted quite firmly for the Liturgy of the Word to come early in the service, but this is mainly because their marriage service is set in the context of a eucharist.

3. The Liturgy of Marriage

The Roman Catholics propose that the homily which ends the Liturgy of the Word should be followed by an invitation to the couple to exchange their consent. The exchange of consent is, of course, enshrined in the vows.

At present, in England, non-Anglicans are required to use an archaic and legalized form of the vow and it is a matter of simple injustice that they are not allowed to use a version similar to the one in the ASB.

This archaic vow, required by law to be in this form, is in the following form if an Authorized Person is present to register the marriage:

'I,__, do take thee, __,
to be my wedded *wife/husband.*'

but takes this form if a Registrar is present:

'I call upon these persons here present
to witness that I, __,
do take thee, __,
to be my lawful wedded *wife/husband.*'

Thus a modern language service has to have this archaic wording embedded in the middle of it, whatever the authors of the rest of the service have done.

The vow may be read or recited by the couple or may be repeated after the priest in the traditional way. There is also a question and answer form of the vow where all the bride and groom say is 'I do'. The giving away has (nearly) disappeared, it just about creeps into a rubric as a possibility.

After the vows, there is a ratification of consent by the priest, declaring that the couple are now married. Applause and kissing are permitted at this point. Certainly this is a point at which something spectacular needs to happen - maybe a fanfare of trumpets. The ASB's acclamations (included in the Roman Catholic proposals for the first time) could fulfil this function if they were led boldly and loudly. Next follows the signing of registers, a state parallel to the priest's declaration that the couple are married. It is therefore strongly urged that the registration takes place here and not at the end of the service.

The next section of the service comprises a collection of illustrative rituals and this

---

1 In his chapter in Michael Perham (ed.), *Liturgy for a New Century* (SPCK 1991)

includes the exchange of rings. Putting it here is an attempt to help people avoid seeing the exchange of rings as the point of marriage. As well as rings, the couple may exchange gifts and even when only one ring is used there are words for the one receiving it to say, so that there is mutuality even in such a case.

Each family may have lit a family candle earlier in the service (and they may have been used at engagement rituals). At this point the couple may light their own wedding candle from the two family candles, these latter then being extinguished. A small and suitable gift may be presented to the couple by a representative of the parish. As we saw above, the candle and the gift reappear in the blessing of the home.

There then follows the nuptial blessing and several forms are given. There has been an attempt to move away from the prayer being focussed on the bride but this has not been as thoroughgoing as it might have been. However, it is at least clear what the nuptial blessing is. In the ASB, there is the blessing of the couple after the priest has declared that they are husband and wife but there is also a prayer in the appendix of possible intercessions (para. 35) which looks like a classic nuptial blessing. I wonder how often it is ever used?[1]

In the draft Roman Catholic proposals, the liturgy of marriage ends with the prayers. A significant feature of this is that the couple are encouraged to pray aloud themselves. The rubric in my copy of the draft (June 1990) says 'It is most desirable that the couple say together a brief prayer of their own composition. Any such prayer should be clearly audible to the congregation.' A selection of possible prayers follows, but couples may compose their own. There is also opportunity for parents and/or members of the two families to pray in a similar way. General intercessions are to be used as well.

4. Liturgy of the Eucharist

The liturgy of the eucharist is straightforwardly derived from the Roman Missal. There is proper material suitable for weddings for the presentation of the gifts, the prayer after communion and the blessing and dismissal.

The significance of these Roman Catholic Draft Proposals is that they make concrete some of the thinking about wedding services which has been developing in recent years. Anglicans (and others) can learn from them ways of adapting existing marriage liturgies to reflect such thinking. We could also be more aware of developments elsewhere in the Christian Church. The Book of Alternative Services from the Canadian Anglican Church has a eucharistic prayer specially for weddings.[2] The Baptist Service Book has quite a long nuptial blessing, and the congregation may join in part of it.[3] I will list some of the ways in which this adapting of existing rites can be done in the final chapter.

---

1 Exeter diocese asked the House of Bishops in 1990 what constituted a nuptial blessing and who may give it. Women deacons might have been particularly in view in the latter part of the question and the Bishops' resultant guidelines address this, but they admit there is no clear view as to what a nuptial blessing is (at least for Anglicans). See *News of Liturgy* 212 (August 1992). pp.10f and issue 213 (Sept. 1992) p.8.
2 Canadian *BAS* p. 536-538.
3 *Patterns and Prayers for Christian Worship* pp. 129f.

4.
Symbolism

It is becoming customary to begin any discussion of symbolism in marriage with a distressing account of the secular symbolism we already have. Stevenson writes:

'A friend recently wrote to me after looking after a group of parishes in the North for a few weeks. Having spent most of his ministry in non-parochial work, he was naturally looking forward to encountering the scene at what is sometimes referred to as "the coal-face" of the church. In the course of those few weeks, he had to preside over three weddings, and he was appalled at the way things had changed. Being prone to slight exaggeration, he described the service as "a more or less equal mixture of the Chelsea Flower Show, Trooping the Colour, the Miss World Competition, and a film company on location...." I wonder if the current fad for going over the top at weddings is not really in part a commentary on the rather dismal liturgies that we have used at marriages for some time.'[1]

One of the hallmarks of Stevenson's work is his advocating the use of new symbolism in marriage rites. Using his historical treatment, Stevenson has produced a list of almost every conceivable piece of symbolism associated with marriage rites.[2] The impression he gives is that he would like to see a lot of this historical symbolism revived in modern marriage services. The question which is begged is how far much of it would work, having been transferred from one culture to another. Few places in Britain seem to have experimented with this and, when I asked Stevenson about this,[3] he explained that he had simply produced a list of symbolism to get people started in thinking about this area because we really are starting at ground level with this in the Church of England. In this chapter, therefore, I will simply list much of this possible symbolism in the hope that someone, somewhere might begin to experiment with it. It is possible to find fresh symbols and it is always necessary to remember that a service should not be overloaded with symbolism and that some things will work in one parish and not in others, often depending on the prevailing local culture.

1. Exchange of Rings
This is one symbol with which we are familiar in weddings and is a symbol which continues after the wedding service, indeed throughout the couple's lives.

2. Precious Coins
This is an old Lincolnshire (and Irish) custom in which the groom gives the bride precious coins after he has put the ring on her finger. It is perhaps a relic of the gifts of gold and silver in the Sarum and 1549 rites. It could be adapted into the couple exchanging gifts.

3. Incense
Some churches are in danger of overdoing incense (like chips, it goes with everything)

---

1 *Liturgy for a New Century* pp. 59f.
2 *To Join Together* pp. 194ff.
3 In a queue in a sandwich shop near Eaton Square, London.

while other churches would regard it as tantamount to a conversion to Rome. Incense indicates a solemn intercession and so could be used at the nuptial blessing.

4. Canopy

While many people associate the use of a canopy, spread over a couple at a wedding with Judaism, it is a symbol found in Swedish Lutheranism as well. It is symbolic of God's presence, 'covering' the couple. The canopy could be made by the friends and family of the couple or by the church congregation. Alternatively, a church could have one canopy which it used for all weddings. The canopy is supported on poles and is in place throughout the service. It could be decorated with suitable Christian/wedding motifs.

5. Crowning

It is common in the East for couples to be crowned as part of a wedding service. Metal crowns are held above the bride and groom's heads by attendants and this symbolises the special grace God gives in marriage. In some cultures, it may have overtones of this being the couple's special day on which, probably for the only time in their lives, they are treated as royalty. The crowns need not be made of metal, and Stevenson suggests using crowns made from flowers.[1]

6. Anointing

This Coptic custom speaks of marriage as a Christian vocation and there is an obvious link with anointing in baptism, confirmation and ordination. This is one piece of symbolism which is fairly easily introduced. I know of one inner-London parish which anoints couples when they come to book the wedding. In the marriage service itself, anointing could take place at the nuptial blessing or maybe early in the service, to show that both bride and groom have come to accept their new vocation of marriage.

7. Binding

This is perhaps the strangest symbol to British eyes. It is an old Spanish practice and involves binding the couple together using a form of lassoo. Nowadays, this has been transferred out of the marriage rite itself:

> 'Older Spanish custom placed this ceremony within the nuptial Mass. Usually it takes place nowadays at the reception afterwards. North Americans... prefer such a 'binding' during the liturgy itself, when the formality of the occasion would make it easy to cope with this many-levelled symbolism. Historically it belongs with the nuptial blessing.'[2]

Binding may encourage inappropriate thoughts of sexual proclivity among some British wedding parties, but it makes the point that some symbol of the two becoming one might be helpful. The use of family candles is an attempt to do this, but may not be the best way forward (see below). It is possible for binding to be carried out

---

1 On crowning in the East, see J. Meyendorff *Marriage: An Orthodox Perspective* (St. Vladimir's Seminary Press, 1984) pp. 37ff.
2 Stevenson *To Join Together* pp. 197f.

by family and friends and there are ways of performing the ritual which are dignified and help the symbol to make the right impression.

There is, of course, a 'binding' ritual to be found in many Anglican wedding services: binding the couples' hands with a stole. Like much of what happens in a wedding ceremony, this may not be seen by the majority of the congregation. If it is done, it is worth doing visibly.

8. Candles

Candles are becoming very popular in liturgy. *The Promise of His Glory* is full of candles and it is quite common to see candles used at baptism in even the most protestant churches nowadays. Wedding candles are already in use in some places. Are they appropriate?

At a wedding, the candles are used to symbolize two families uniting in the union of the couple. It may be objected that lights and candles should be reserved to symbolize God's presence, to recall Jesus' words about being the Light of the World and the calling of Christians to be lights in a dark world. I have reservations about their use in weddings for two reasons. One is that candles do not seem to me to be an appropriate symbol of the two becoming one flesh and the other is that, if we overdo candles as a symbol, they are in danger of losing their power as a symbol. Familiarity breeds contempt. Maybe a practising Christian couple would want to light one candle from the Paschal candle (a marital equivalent of a baptismal candle) as a sign of their vocation/resolve to shine as lights for Christ in their marriage.

This would also link their marriage with Paschal themes and be a statement that they, as Christians, want to live every part of their lives in the light of the cross and resurrection. This marital candle could be relit at anniversaries, the blessing of a new home etc.

9. Laying on of Hands

This would occur at the nuptial blessing, and I know of a few Anglican clergy who do this already. Again, it provides a link with such activities as confirmation and ordination and speaks of God's grace and the couple's commissioning. It is perhaps the easiest of all new symbols to introduce.

Several comments can be made about this whole area of symbolism in marriage:

(a) It would be foolish to put all or many of the new symbols into one service. This would lead to severe overloading. Some symbols could be used at times other than the marriage service itself (as for example the Hispanic binding at the wedding reception). It is important to be highly selective and to use what is appropriate to the circumstances and the local culture.

(b) The local culture is very important. It is important to remember that Britain does not have one uniform culture. Different cultures can co-exist alongside each other in the same place and it is very common to find great cultural differences within a few miles. There may be some local customs which could be used or adapted at weddings. An obvious example of this happening already is a guard of honour when one of the couple is a member of the armed forces.

(c) Be creative. While it would be possible to invest in commercial equipment to introduce some of the new symbolism, it is better if items are produced by the congregation or the families concerned. This stops attempts at new symbolism looking odd or overdone. A home-made canopy, embroidered with designs appropriate to the couple would work better than something bought from a catalogue.

(d) The symbols mentioned above are illustrative (and therefore secondary) and should not usurp the place of whatever we think is the central act of the marriage rite. Symbols may be more than illustrative, but I do not feel that the ones in the list in this chapter fit easily into any other category.

(e) Symbols should therefore remain as symbols and not be excuses for mini sermons. Stevenson puts this point well:

> '...they must not be introduced by a long and specious explanation by a celebrant who trusts neither the liturgy to do its job nor the congregation to relate to a welcome piece of non-verbal liturgy in a wordy world.'[1]

(f) Having said all this, and while I remain enthusiastic for introducing new symbols into the marriage service, I am not entirely convinced that they will displace the current tarting up of the service which people like Stevenson complain about. I suspect that couples will still have chimney sweeps around for good luck, elaborate processions of bridesmaids and so on. It is true, however, that the service as it stands at the moment lacks a great deal of specifically Christian symbolism. This is not surprising if it developed out of Roman (and therefore pagan/secular) weddings. It may be argued that many couples who come for marriage are not practising Christians and so such symbolism would be inappropriate. What we need is a marriage service which is fully Christian in its symbolism and theology, but which is pastorally flexible. We should not be shy of advocating the Christian dimensions to marriage. This may cause some couples to think more deeply about their view of marriage and maybe to adopt a more fully Christian view. This is not to argue that the church should become withdrawn from the world in such a way that those who do not have a robust and active Christian faith would not be welcome to come for weddings, but simply that we should be honest about ourselves as a *Christian church*.

---

1 *To Join Together* p. 199.

5.
The Wider Context

Much of what I have written so far has been concerned with the wedding service itself or other services which may form part of a set of phased rites. There are other issues, of a wider nature which need addressing.

1. Ecumenism

When one partner is a member of one denomination and the other partner is a member of another, there is often great discussion as to how the wedding service can reflect this. Often it is reduced to 'inviting the other minister to read the lesson or lead the prayers'. The situation is further complicated if we ask which parts of the ASB service are legally necessary for the marriage to be valid. The register says that the couple were married according to the rites and ceremonies of the Church of England. What are these rites and ceremonies?

Further complications arise where one partner is a practising member of one denomination and the other partner is a non-practising member of another. What also about members of an L.E.P. who have no particular denominational allegiance (because perhaps they have both become Christians through that church)? The usual compromise seems to be to use an Anglican service. We urgently need a truly ecumenical one.[1] In these days of liturgical borrowing and swopping between communions, such a service need not be very difficult to produce. (The Roman Catholic draft proposals use a certain amount of material from the ASB).

2. Inter-Faith Weddings

Apart from the pastoral issues arising from the wedding of a nominal or practising Christian to a member of another faith, there are liturgical issues too. Can we include material from non-Christian liturgies? How do we cope with theological differences (e.g. in the understanding of marriage)? Does it make a difference if the non-Christian partner is not actively practising his/her faith?

There are almost no guidelines in this area. The Inter-Faith Consultative Group's *Multi-Faith Worship?* does not address this issue (but was presumably not asked or expected to), though its conclusions probably point to the inappropriateness of holding a fully Christian service in such circumstances as well as to the difficuties for Christians of using a service which contains material drawn from other faiths.[2]

3. Secular Weddings

We already have the blessing of a civil marriage as a Church of England option. There are regular calls for all weddings in Britain to be performed at a Register Office fol-

---

1 There is an example of a north American ecumenical service in Stevenson and Searle *op. cit.* pp. 239ff.
2 *Multi-Faith Worship?* (CHP 1992), see for example pp. 51-59. David Bookless suggests that only neutral buildings be used for interfaith worship, and this would preclude weddings, since at present, only licensed places of worship (and Register Offices) may be used. See Bookless', *Interfaith Worship and Christian Truth* (Grove Worship Series 117), especially p.22.

lowed by a church service if desired. This is the pattern in France (and elsewhere) and it at least has the advantage that the church service is not 'the legal bit' and so the text of it can vary considerably. Such a practice would raise the question of the moment of marriage again in that the couple had exchanged consent at the Register Office but had not received a nuptial blessing, so is it appropriate for them to walk down the aisle together? My own answer would be that they should be encouraged to come to church as a married couple and have some kind of entrance procession such as that described in chapter three. They are married in the eyes of the society in which they live and so it seems appropriate for the church to treat them as a married couple.

Many couples seek a church wedding because they want a beautiful building in which to be married. One is tempted to say that some of them just want a good background for photographs. Undoubtedly, it is good pastoral practice to meet such couples where they are rather than condemn them as soon as such thoughts are expressed. However, changes in the law in England might mean that weddings could take place in all sorts of places other than churches and Register Offices, as is currently the case. Stately homes might be obvious choices instead of churches. What is a Christian minister to do if she is invited to officiate in a stately home or at the Oldham Lyceum[1] (which has always struck me as a suitably decorous place for a wedding)?

4. Marriage and Reality

When I have spoken about the Roman Catholic proposals for England and Wales to various groups such as clergy chapters, the response has often been that they are removed from reality and too romantic (in the sense of not being sufficiently realistic). I personally feel that this is not entirely just, but there remains the fact that marriage rites generally do not address the reality and fears of getting married.

Questions go through the couple's mind in the run-up to the wedding (and doubtless during the wedding itself) such as 'will this marriage last?' Most couples will know people whose marriages have broken up; will theirs be any different? (I find the couples who most insist on a 1662 service are the ones where one partner has been divorced. I suspect that they want the old service as a kind of folk religion guarantee that this marriage will last if they 'do it properly' by having the old words).

Other issues might be the existence of children from previous marriages, adjusting to living together, coping with sexual relations (in a culture which seems to make this the be-all and end-all of marriage) and perhaps the uncertainty of life in general - the vows speak of sticking together through illness, poverty etc.

I find I can touch on some of these issues in wedding preparation and in the address at the wedding service. It would be good to work at texts which took these issues seriously. Wedding preparation materials which integrate well with a flexible (and fuller) liturgy would be a tremendous help - the wedding service address is not the best opportunity to deal at length with these issues.

Staged (or phased) rites would help here because the wedding service itself would

---

1 For those readers who have never visited Oldham, the Lyceum is an elegantly restored Victorian building, owned by the Borough Council, normally used for training events and by the schools' music service and containing an impressive staircase and sumptuous rooms. Readers can probably think of their own local examples.

not have to carry all the hopes and fears of the couple (and their families and friends). Much of the apprehension about getting married and setting up home together could be handled in preparatory rites and domestic issues obviously fit with the blessing of a home. Even here, there is the need for the texts and for the services in general to make an attempt at being realistic rather then simply painting a uniformly rosy picture.

For example, the Roman Catholic proposals for a rite of reconciliation which I have seen include scope for confession of sin, including the possibility of the couple (or others) confessing to each other. There is a balance to be kept here between declaring God's forgiveness and a new start in the marriage relationship and the realistic realization that things will probably not improve dramatically overnight. There is a need for continuing pastoral support and the seeking of God's grace. The service does acknowledge this latter emphasis, but maybe not as strongly as it might. It is, nonetheless, a difficult balance to achieve liturgically.

There are some very good marriage preparation materials available now which do encourage couples to face the realities of being married,[1] but few, if any, of them attempt to give the preparation a liturgical context. Couples will vary in how appropriate they would find this, but this is an area which those who prepare couples for marriage could explore.

6.
What can Anglicans do now?

Most of this booklet has been suggesting paths towards revising the ASB marriage service. Such a revision is just coming on to the Liturgical Commission's agenda at the moment. It would be most helpful if changes were introduced gradually, maybe by some experimentation now with what we already have. One of the laws of liturgical development enunciated by Anton Baumstark was that liturgy is most resistant to change on special occasions. Certainly Anglican marriage rites have changed little since Sarum. More radical changes, such as those suggested in this booklet, will need to be introduced gradually and experimented with. This process can begin in some of the following ways:

1. Encourage couples who are practising Christians to have their wedding service in the context of a eucharist (which was Cranmer's intention). This would link human marriage with God's redeeming acts and demonstrate that marriage is one of the things for which we give thanks. There are, of course, problems associated with having weddings in a eucharistic context - not least of the fact that many guests may not wish to communicate. This, however, is not the problem it is often made out to be because the eucharist should be the natural context for Christian

---

1 See for example Margaret Stevens *Preparing Couples for Marriage* (Grove Pastoral Series 28.)

worship; and can we really deny a Christian couple a eucharistic setting for their wedding if the eucharist is a focal point in their spiritual lives anyway?[1]

2. Begin to introduce the idea of phased rites. For example, more could be made of praying for couples when their Banns are read out. It could be made clear that clergy are willing to say prayers in a new home. Marriage vows could be renewed and anniversaries could be celebrated liturgically.

3. Experiment with new symbolism. Anointing and hand-laying are obvious candidates. Some situations may enable other experiments to be tried.

4. Try to get away from the event being seen as 'the bride's day'. The couple could enter church together. Both partners could be 'given away' or have sponsors. Prayers should be for both of them and not just the bride.

5. Introduce a more solid nuptial blessing. The prayer in the ASB Appendix could be used or some could be written afresh. It should be modelled on the eucharistic prayer and focus on thanksgiving to God for his blessings. Since the prayers are to some degree optional in the ASB structure (i.e. there is flexibility as to which prayers are used), it should be possible to include more fulsome nuptial blessings at this point. We do not even need to write our own - we could borrow material from the new Baptist service book.[2]

6. Introduce a note of reality by including children of former marriages (as bridesmaids/page boys or get them to read lessons). The Anglican Church in New Zealand includes a question to the children just after the consent. It follows a similar question to the parents, and asks the children to support the couple in their marriage.[3] The address can touch on some of these issues, as can the prayers (in asking God's grace for the couple as they begin their married life).

7. Encourage greater participation. At the moment, the congregation has nothing to say apart from the opening response to the celebrant's greeting and the acclamations in the middle of the service. A question asking the congregation to support the couple and a similar question to the respective families could easily be introduced into the service. The congregation could present the couple with a gift. The couple themselves could read or recite the vows (though this is probably asking a lot of nervous people) and they could compose and/or read their own prayers. Perhaps the Peace could be used (after the declaration that the couple are husband and wife or after the signing of registers, if this happens in the middle of the service).

8. By putting the registration close to the declaration of marriage and by having the ministry of the word at the beginning of the service, certain theological points can be made (the registration is the legal counterpart of the declaration and the couple are getting married in the context of salvation history).

1 See for example Colin Buchanan *The Heart of Sunday Worship* (Grove Worship Series 121).
2 *Patterns and Prayers* pp.129f.
3 *A New Zealand Prayer Book* p. 786.